Understanding the Coronavirus

The Search

for Treatments and a Vaccine

Margaret J. Goldstein

Lerner Publications ◆ Minneapolis

Lerner Publications Company
An imprint of Lerner Publishing Group, Inc.
241 First Avenue North
Minneapolis, MN 55401 USA

For reading levels and more information, look up this title
at www.lernerbooks.com.

Main body text set in Adrianna Regular.
Typeface provided by Chank.

Library of Congress Cataloging-in-Publication Data

Names: Goldstein, Margaret J., author.
Title: The search for treatments and a vaccine / Margaret J. Goldstein.
Description: Minneapolis : Lerner Publications , [2022] | Series: Searchlight books - understanding the coronavirus | Includes bibliographical references and index. | Audience: Ages 8–11 | Audience: Grades 2–3 | Summary: "As COVID-19 raged around the world in 2020, scientists undertook an unprecedented effort to create effective treatments and vaccines. Learn how medical professionals fought back against a deadly disease" —Provided by publisher.
Identifiers: LCCN 2021009283 (print) | LCCN 2021009284 (ebook) | ISBN 9781728428512 (library binding) | ISBN 9781728431482 (paperback) | ISBN 9781728430768 (ebook)
Subjects: LCSH: COVID-19 (Disease)—Treatment—Juvenile literature. | COVID-19 (Disease)—Research. | Vaccination—Juvenile literature. | Epidemics—Juvenile literature.
Classification: LCC RA644.C67 G6475 2022 (print) | LCC RA644.C67 (ebook) | DDC 614.5/92414—dc23

LC record available at https://lccn.loc.gov/2021009283
LC ebook record available at https://lccn.loc.gov/2021009284

Manufactured in the United States of America
1-49388-49492-4/26/2021

Table of Contents

Chapter 1

SICK TIME

In late 2019, media outlets reported that a new virus was making people sick. The first cases were found in China, but international travelers soon carried the virus to other nations. Scientists named it SARS-CoV-2. It was a type of coronavirus, and it caused a disease called COVID-19.

COVID-19 is a contagious disease. Infected people release virus-filled droplets into the air when they sneeze, cough, talk, and breathe. Someone standing nearby might inhale the droplets and get infected too. The droplets might land on a surface, such as a doorknob or a computer keyboard. If someone else touches that surface and then touches their own eyes, nose, or mouth, the virus can enter their body.

A virus can spread through the air when a person sneezes or coughs.

The coronavirus mainly attacks the respiratory system. Infection begins in the throat and moves down to the lungs. The virus causes different symptoms in different people. Some people get body aches, a fever, a runny nose, or a cough. Others have headaches or feel extremely tired. Some people with COVID-19 lose their sense of taste or smell. Others have no symptoms at all.

A fever is a common symptom of COVID-19.

STEM Spotlight

You can take precautions to avoid getting COVID-19 from others. Avoid crowded places, such as stores, restaurants, and big gatherings. If you do spend time with others, stand at least 6 feet (2 m) away from them. Wear a face mask over your nose and mouth to stop the virus from spreading. Wash your hands regularly or use hand sanitizer to remove virus particles on your skin.

The coronavirus does the most damage when it enters the lungs. When that happens, it can be hard to breathe. The lungs might not be able to supply oxygen to other organs, such as the kidneys or liver. Without enough oxygen, these organs can stop working, and the person can die.

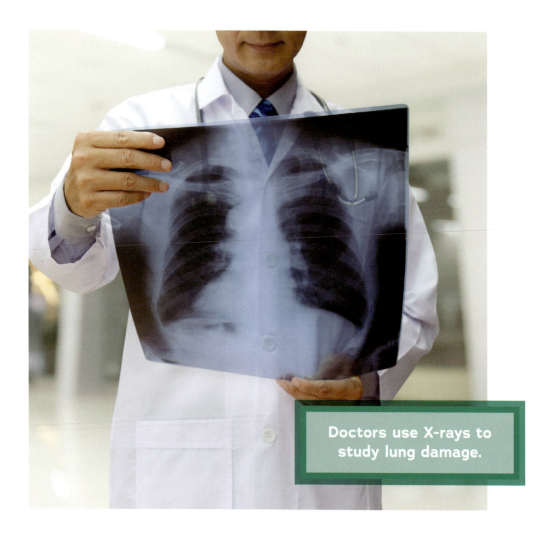

Doctors use X-rays to study lung damage.

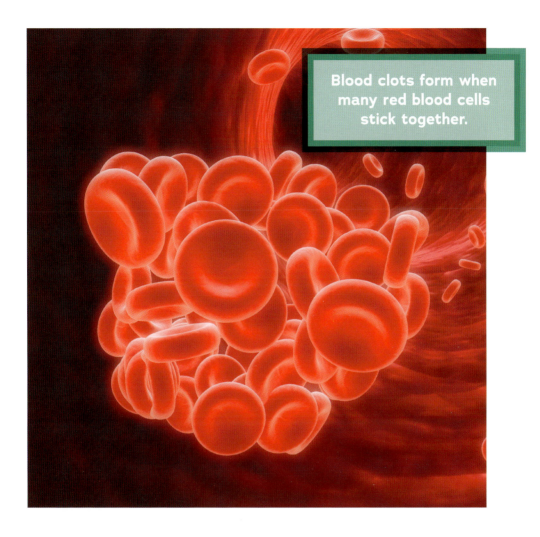

Blood clots form when many red blood cells stick together.

The virus might also invade other parts of the body. It might attack the heart, blood vessels, or other organs. Many COVID-19 patients develop blood clots, which can lead to strokes or death. Elderly people and those with diabetes, high blood pressure, or other health problems are most likely to get severely ill with COVID-19.

A Race against Time

Throughout 2020, COVID-19 spread from person to person. The outbreak became a pandemic, infecting people all over the world. As more and more people got sick, doctors searched for treatments and medicines. Medical researchers searched for a vaccine that would keep people from getting sick with COVID-19.

A PATIENT RECEIVES A COVID-19 TEST AT AN OUTDOOR TESTING SITE.

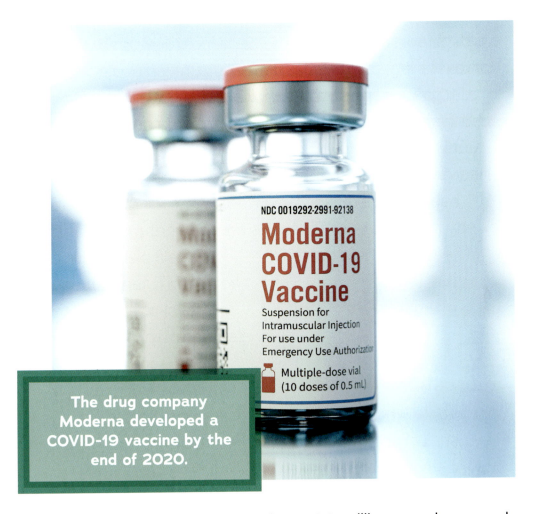

The drug company Moderna developed a COVID-19 vaccine by the end of 2020.

By January 2021, more than 100 million people around the world had tested positive for COVID-19. More than two million had died. But good news was on the horizon. Several drug companies had created COVID-19 vaccines. Vaccination programs began in many nations. Vaccines offer hope that the COVID-19 pandemic will finally come to an end.

Chapter 2

COVID-19 CARE

Most people who get COVID-19 have mild symptoms. They usually recover on their own, without medical help. Doctors say they can take store-bought medicines to relieve symptoms such as body aches, a stuffy nose, or a sore throat.

People can pass the virus to others even if they don't have symptoms. For this reason, doctors recommend that people who test positive for COVID-19 stay home for about two weeks, even if they don't feel sick.

The Most At-Risk Patients

Some people become seriously ill with COVID-19. They may have chest pains or trouble breathing. Medical professionals recommend that people with these symptoms go to the emergency room for treatment.

Some COVID-19 patients need to be treated at hospitals for respiratory problems.

Emily Charvat

Nurse Emily Charvat takes care of COVID-19 patients at a hospital in Omaha, Nebraska. She works ten-hour shifts, often dashing from room to room, helping patients in a life-or-death struggle with COVID-19. To protect herself from infection, she wears a plastic gown over her hospital scrubs. She also wears gloves, a face mask, and a hard plastic face shield. The job can be exhausting and heartbreaking, but Charvat thinks of herself as a warrior in the fight against COVID-19.

Nurses like Charvat have to wear personal protective equipment when treating patients.

In hospitals, doctors use many tools to help COVID-19 patients. They give extra oxygen to those having trouble breathing. Some patients get oxygen through a plastic mask that fits over the nose and mouth. Others need a ventilator. This machine pumps air through a tube, directly into a patient's windpipe. The ventilator helps the patient breathe until their lungs are strong enough to work on their own. Another helpful technique is to lay patients facedown, on their stomachs. This position relieves pressure on the lungs, so breathing is easier.

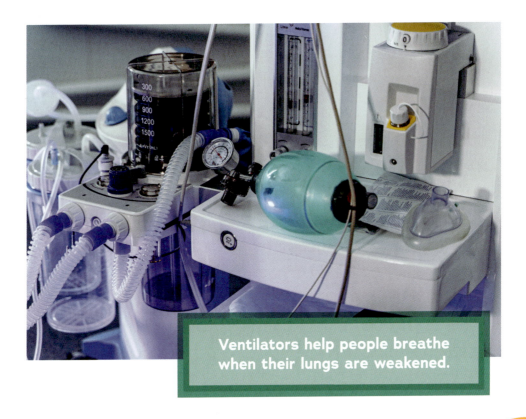

Ventilators help people breathe when their lungs are weakened.

Remdesivir has helped some patients recover from COVID-19.

Doctors also give medicines to COVID-19 patients. Because the virus attacks different patients in different ways, doctors tailor medicines to each patient's needs. Some medicines treat damage in the lungs. Others help prevent blood clots. A drug called remdesivir works by damaging the virus that causes COVID-19. Medical researchers are studying other medicines to find the ones that work best.

Chapter 3

A SHOT IN THE ARM

Medicines are important in treating COVID-19, but vaccines are better because they keep people from getting sick in the first place. Vaccines work by triggering the body's immune system.

The immune system is the human body's defense against disease. When a virus or other germ infects the body, the immune system goes into action. It fights the invader with antibodies and special cells. Some of these cells even "remember" the invader. If the same germ enters the body again, the memory cells recognize it right away. They alert the rest of the immune system. Antibodies and other defenses get to work much more quickly than the first time. This quick response defeats the invader before it can make the person sick.

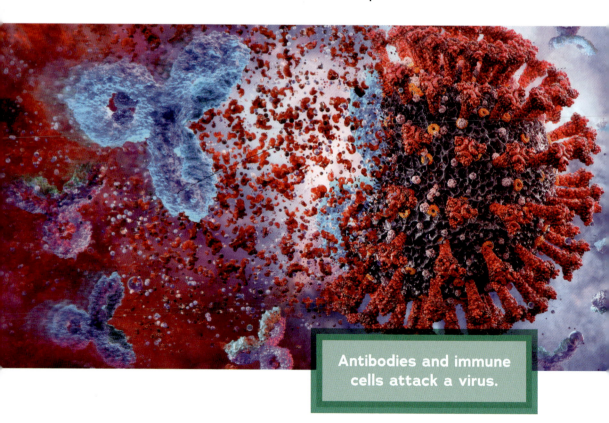

Antibodies and immune cells attack a virus.

DOCTORS PREVENT MEASLES AND OTHER DISEASES USING VACCINES.

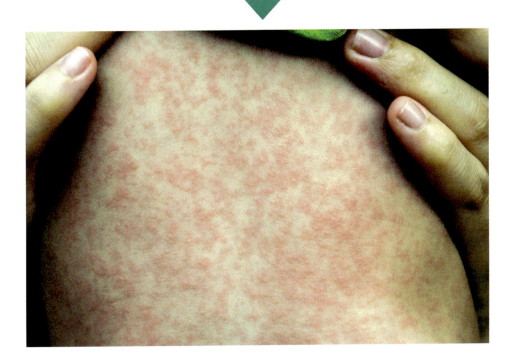

Vaccines activate the immune system too. Vaccines are harmless, but the body thinks they are dangerous invaders. If you get a vaccine for measles, for instance, your immune system will respond by creating antibodies, memory cells, and other defenses against measles. Later, if the real measles virus enters your body, your immune system will be able to quickly defend against it. You won't get sick with measles.

A New Kind of Vaccine

Scientists make different types of vaccines. Some are made from weakened or killed versions of viruses or bacteria. Others are made from substances found in viruses or bacteria. The COVID-19 vaccine is a new type of vaccine. It contains messenger RNA (mRNA). This substance is normally found inside viruses, but the mRNA in the COVID-19 vaccine comes from a laboratory.

STEM Spotlight

Viruses are tiny particles that infect living things. They latch onto living cells and work their way inside. Once a virus is inside a cell, it uses material in the cell to reproduce, or make copies of itself. As the virus reproduces, it damages the cell. This damage leads to illness. Different kinds of viruses attack different kinds of cells. The coronavirus mainly attacks cells in the human respiratory system, but it can also attack other cells.

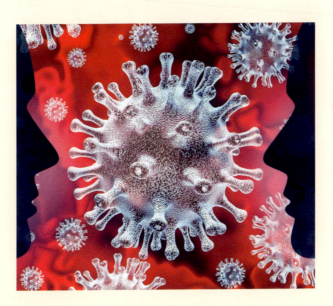

The mRNA in the COVID-19 vaccine is like an instruction manual. It tells a body's cells to make a certain kind of protein. It is the same protein found on the outside of the coronavirus, but it is harmless instead of dangerous. The immune system doesn't know the protein is harmless, though. It thinks it's a real coronavirus, so it builds up defenses. Those defenses will provide protection if the real virus attacks later on.

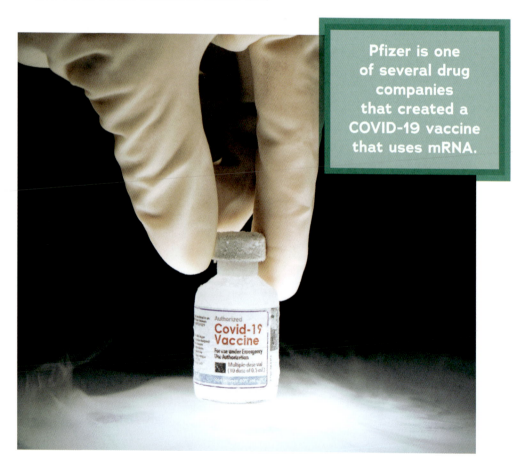

Pfizer is one of several drug companies that created a COVID-19 vaccine that uses mRNA.

Chapter 4

QUESTIONS AND ANSWERS

In December 2020, health agencies around the world began vaccinating for COVID-19. Wealthier nations, such as the United States and the United Kingdom, were the first ones to start vaccination. Other nations have less money to purchase and distribute vaccines, so the World Health Organization and other agencies have stepped in to help. They have launched a program called COVAX. It provides funds, equipment, training, and other tools for vaccine distribution in poor nations.

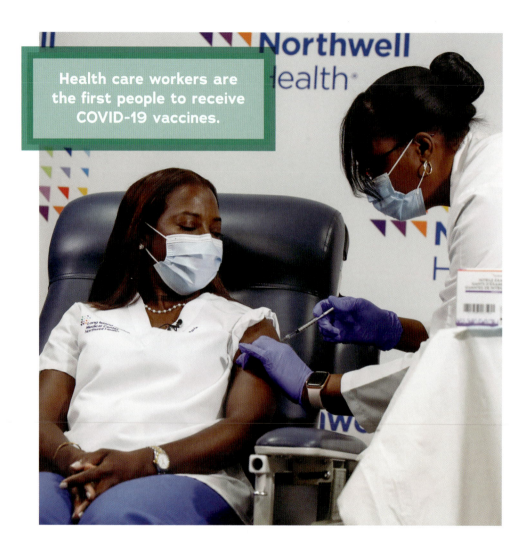

Health care workers are the first people to receive COVID-19 vaccines.

Vaccinated people will not get sick with COVID-19, but scientists don't know how long protection will last. The virus is changing. Scientists will have to change the vaccine too. People might need a new COVID-19 vaccine every year or every few years.

A COVID-19 vaccine will keep you from getting sick if the virus enters your body. But will the vaccine prevent you from passing the virus to others? Scientists aren't sure. Eventually, when most people have been vaccinated, the virus will spread more slowly. Until then, scientists say people should still wear masks and practice social distancing in public places, even after vaccination.

PEOPLE CONTINUE TO PRACTICE SOCIAL DISTANCING AND WEAR MASKS.

Dr. Kizzmekia Corbett

The push to create a COVID-19 vaccine involved teams of scientists around the world. Dr. Kizzmekia Corbett (*below, right*) is one of these scientists. A specialist in viruses and the immune system, she joined the Vaccine Research Center at the National Institutes of Health (NIH), a US government agency, in 2014. In 2020, she and her colleagues at NIH teamed up with the drug company Moderna to make one of the first effective COVID-19 vaccines. Corbett has taken a lead role in encouraging other Americans to get vaccinated.

More Viruses

SARS-CoV-2 took the world by surprise. It was a brand-new virus that scientists had never seen before. Scientists say that other new viruses will emerge in the future. The lessons of COVID-19 will help us fight them.

Sandra Lindsay, a registered nurse in Long Island, was the first American to receive the COVID-19 vaccine.

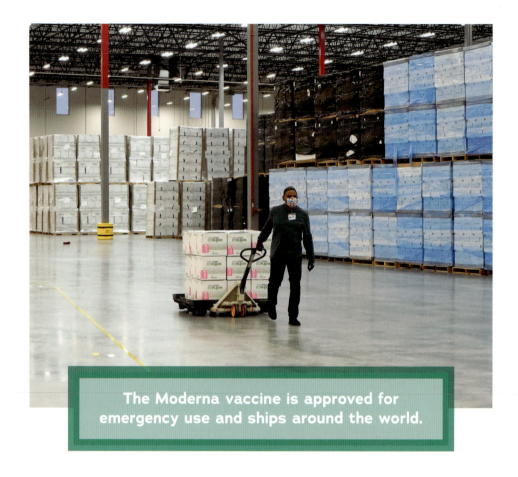

The Moderna vaccine is approved for emergency use and ships around the world.

Because of the pandemic, people have learned the importance of social distancing, handwashing, and mask wearing. Because of COVID-19, scientists have learned to make vaccines in record time. And medical researchers have discovered better ways to treat sick people. By remembering the lessons learned from fighting the coronavirus, we can have a healthier future.

Important Dates

December 2019   News agencies in China announce an outbreak of a new virus.

January 2020   A man in Washington State is the first American found to have COVID-19.

March 2020   The US Centers for Disease Control and Prevention (CDC) reports more than 18,000 COVID-19 cases in the United States.

May 2020   The US government launches Operation Warp Speed to fast-track development of a COVID-19 vaccine.

October 2020   The US Food and Drug Administration allows the use of the drug remdesivir to treat COVID-19 patients.

November 2020   The drug company Moderna announces that it has developed an effective COVID-19 vaccine.

December 2020   Nurse Sandra Lindsay is the first American to get the COVID-19 vaccine.

Glossary

antibodies: proteins produced by the immune system to fight infection

contagious: able to spread from person to person

coronavirus: a virus whose surface is covered by spiky projections

immune system: a network of cells, tissues, and proteins that defend the body against disease

pandemic: a worldwide outbreak of a disease

positive: having an infection or illness, as indicated by a test result

protein: a substance in cells that does a particular job

respiratory system: the body's breathing organs, including the nose, windpipe, and lungs

social distancing: keeping a certain amount of space between yourself and others, usually 6 feet (2 m), to prevent the spread of disease from person to person

vaccine: a substance that prepares the immune system to fight off an invader, such as a virus

virus: a tiny particle that can infect living cells and cause disease

Learn More

Coronavirus Glossary
> https://kids.nationalgeographic.com/science/article/coronavirus
> -glossary

Doeden, Matt. *The COVID-19 Pandemic*. Minneapolis: Lerner Publications, 2021.

Hudak, Heather C. *COVID-19*. New York: Av2, 2021.

Immune System
> https://www.ducksters.com/science/biology/immune_system.php

Stocker, Shannon. *Social Distancing*. Ann Arbor, MI: Cherry Lake Publishing, 2021.

Viral Attack
> https://askabiologist.asu.edu/memory-b-cell

Index

Photo Acknowledgments

Image credits: Billion Photos/Shutterstock, p.5; Prostock-studio/Shutterstock, p.6; TORWAISTUDIO/Shutterstock, p.7; TippaPatt/Shutterstock, p.8; SciePro/ZUMA Wire/Shutterstock, p.9; Leon Neal/Getty Images, p.10; guteksk7/Shutterstock, p.11; Pablo Blazquez Dominguez/Stringer/Getty Images, p.13; Boyloso/Daily Express/Hulton Archive/Shutterstock, p.14; Terelyuk/Shutterstock, p.15; Bernard Chantal/Philadelphia Inquirer/MCT/Shutterstock, p.16; Corona Borealis Studio/Atlanta Journal-Constitution/TNS/Shutterstock, p.18; phichet chaiyabin/Shutterstock, p.19; Karen Ducey/Stringer/Getty Images, p.20; Lightspring/ZUMA Wire/Shutterstock, p.21; myboys.me/Shutterstock, p.22; Pool/Getty Images, p.24; Luis Alvarez/Getty Images, p.25; CNP/AdMedia/SIPA/Newscom, p.26; SMG/ZUMAPRESS/rosiekeystrokes/Newscom, 27; Pool/Getty Images, p.28

Cover: fcafotodigital/Getty Images